STOP
STARING
AT
SCREENS

For Ellie and Finn,
the best part of life offscreen

An Hachette UK Company
www.hachette.co.uk

First published in Great Britain in 2018
by Ilex, a division of
Octopus Publishing Group Ltd
Carmelite House
50 Victoria Embankment
London EC4Y 0DZ
www.octopusbooks.co.uk

Distributed in the US by
Hachette Book Group
1290 Avenue of the Americas
4th and 5th Floors
New York, NY 10104

Distributed in Canada by
Canadian Manda Group
664 Annette St.
Toronto, Ontario, Canada M6S 2C8

Publisher: Roly Allen
Editorial Director: Helen Rochester
Commissioning Editor: Zara Anvari
Managing Editor: Frank Gallaugher
Editor: Jenny Dye
Publishing Assistant:
Stephanie Hetherington
Art Director: Julie Weir
Designer: Ben Gardiner
Production Manager: Caroline Alberti

ISBN 978-1-78157-576-5

A CIP catalogue record for this book
is available from the British Library.

Printed and bound in China
10 9 8 7 6 5 4 3 2 1

STOP STARING AT SCREENS

TANYA GOODIN

FOREWORD BY
Dr Mark Griffiths

A DIGITAL DETOX FOR THE WHOLE FAMILY

ilex

1

P. 14
TIME TO TALK
Learn how to avoid
arguments about
screens, and find
out which aspects of
screen life you must
discuss together.

P. 11
HOW TO USE
THIS BOOK

2

P. 32
TAKING
CONTROL
Set boundaries
around screen time
by fixing times and
places you would like
to make screen-free.

3

P. 50
FINDING
BALANCE
Think about what a
healthy "digital diet"
looks like, and learn
how to recognize when
you're going off course.

4

P. 68

HEALTHY BODIES

Discover what happens to our bodies when we are glued to our screens 24/7 and what healthy habits you can adopt to counter the negative effects.

5

P. 86

HEALTHY MINDS

Boost self-esteem, happiness, and all the things that can suffer when we prioritize our online life at the expense of our off-line one.

6

P. 104

WORK

Become more productive by sharpening up some of the brain skills that excessive screen time is eroding.

7

P. 122

LIFE OFFSCREEN

Find ideas on how to make the most of your time away from screens.

P. 143/144

CONCLUSION/ ACKNOWLEDGMENTS

FOREWORD

For many people, going a few minutes without checking a screen is difficult. Whether you are a parent of teenagers or children who spend a disproportionate amount of time glued to smartphones or gaming consoles, or an adult who constantly checks their emails on laptops or tablets, then this is the book for you.

In the late 1980s and mid-1990s, after I had finished my PhD on slot-machine addiction, I started to research video-game addiction and a new phenomenon that had been labelled "internet addiction." I began to conceptualize the research I was doing on different types of excessive technology use as being psychologically and behaviorally similar, and in 1995 I coined the term "technological addictions" in the title of a paper I published that year. Since then, hundreds of academic papers have been published on various different types of technological addictions, including mobile phone addiction and (more recently) smartphone addiction.

The findings have shown that the majority of individuals with technological addictions are more likely to be addicted to the activities they can do via their computers and smartphones, rather than the internet or the devices themselves. An online gambling addict or an online gaming addict is not addicted to the internet: they are using the internet to feed their addiction to gambling or gaming. The same is true for those who are addicted to online shopping, online sex, or online social networking. In short, most people have addictions *on* their screens rather than *to* them. And the really good news is that most people don't have addictions at all. Yes, they spend a lot of time in front of a screen, but their activity is habitual rather than problematic.

There is now a wealth of research that shows that screen time can be put to educational and therapeutic uses. Online interactivity can allow individuals to experience novelty, curiosity, and challenges that stimulate learning. It is therefore important to consider the content and effects of our screen use, and to bear in mind that time spent on screens does not always have negative consequences.

Every week I receive emails from parents claiming that their sons are addicted to playing online games and that their daughters are addicted to social media. I always ask parents the same three things in relation to their child's screen use. Does it affect their schoolwork? Does it affect their physical education? Does it affect their peer development and interaction? Usually none of these things are affected so if that is the case, there is little serious to worry about when it comes to screen time.

Children notice the behavior of those they see around them, so adults also need to be aware of their own screen use and how it impacts on those closest to them. Too many people fail to appreciate being in the moment and allow themselves to resist the urge to continually log on to their laptops, mobiles, and tablets. Looking at screens can become an almost compulsive behavior because of what psychologists have termed "FOMO" (fear of missing out), which refers to the anxiety that an interesting event may be happening elsewhere online.

This self-help book is for the millions of people who habitually use electronic devices in this way, and it gives great examples of how some technology-free time can benefit individuals and their family around them. It is a book that is suggestive and not prescriptive. The world is a much better place due to online connectivity, and the strategies you'll find here are about getting more balance in your life and reconnecting with your family face-to-face rather than only interacting online.

Dr Mark Griffiths
Distinguished Professor of Behavioral Addiction
Director, International Gaming Research Unit
Nottingham Trent University
Nottingham, UK

HOW TO USE THIS BOOK

The smartphones in our pockets and the tablets and laptops in our homes were designed to make our lives easier. Yet these devices are one of the biggest drivers of family rifts and stress, causing daily bust-ups and ever-escalating rows.

Today's children have grown up with screens at every stage in their lives, from educational apps through to their first smartphones. Meanwhile, their parents have been learning about screens at exactly the same time. Both generations are going through a kind of technology adolescence together, learning how to balance the advantages of technology with healthy usage.

Screens have taken up permanent residence in every family space and seem to feature at every occasion: they're in our sitting rooms, at our meal tables, and in our bedrooms; we use them to read, to play music, to distract and entertain ourselves, and to capture precious family memories. We watch each other scrolling mindlessly when we're bored, or escaping into our phones to avoid tricky conversations, with parents and children accusing each other of being the worst culprits. With all the knowledge of the world now at our fingertips, we seem to have forgotten how to get along with each other and don't know how find our way back to a balanced family life.

Every time I host a talk about technology in the home, there are two common cries: "HELP!" and "How can I apply this to my family?" Consider this book your family toolbox for everything that needs fixing about screens at home. Find the way through for your family by following the quiz at the start of each chapter, and tackle problems together and independently using the smart and simple solutions included.

Parents and children will learn together where, when, and how to set new boundaries, and what's practical and workable. Whether you're worried that arguments about technology are escalating or are already at your stress limit, you will find something here for you.

Tanya Goodin

"Consider this book
your family toolbox
for everything that
needs fixing about
screens at home."

CHAPTER

1

TIME TO TALK

The first thing we can do to get control over our devices and reclaim harmony in our homes is talk. Screens are so much a part of our lives that it's inevitable we're talking and arguing about them more and more. But talking doesn't have to lead to tempers getting frayed. Taking the time to talk about what bothers us about our screen use and how we would like things to be different, and even sharing some of the enjoyment of our screen time together, is going to lead to a much happier home than seething in silence or shouting.

One of the issues with talking about screen use is that we tend to do it only when there *is* a problem. Any chance of having a calm and productive conversation is destroyed when an argument has already erupted. Instead, why not make talking about screens something you do regularly and at key stages in your family's life?

- When a child is first given a smartphone or tablet, that's a great opportunity to talk about the online world, what they might find there, and how to behave.

- When a new job means different expectations about responding to emails out of hours, that's another opportunity to talk about how this might affect home life and how everyone will cope.

- When a birthday or Christmas present is a new games console or an intelligent home assistant, that's a chance to talk about what the rules are at home for how (and when) it will be used.

Discover how talking can help your family pinpoint issues caused by screens and come up with solutions together. This section has lots more suggestions to get you started.

DO YOU TALK
MUCH ABOUT SCREENS
AT HOME?

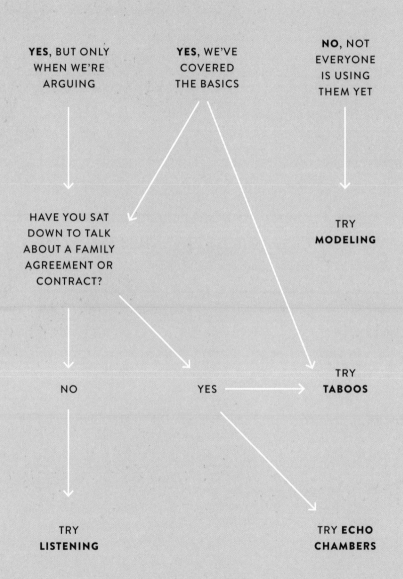

1

LISTENING

"You never *listen* to me!" is a familiar cry in homes everywhere. With screen gadgets taking up more of our time and attention, we can often forget to really listen to each other. So how can we make sure we understand how everyone feels about screen use in the home?

Hearing and listening are two quite different things. We can't help what we hear but we *can* help how we listen. Using a technique called "active listening" is the best way to communicate that you are trying to understand where the other person is coming from. Active listening is not the same as reflective listening where you're just repeating back to the speaker what they said. With active listening, you're trying hard to understand not only the content but also the emotion, body language, and unspoken cues that tell you what's really going on behind the words.

Organize an active listening session to kick off talking about screens at home. Start by picking a good time. Don't try to talk when doors have just been slammed or when anyone is tired or hungry. In all of these situations everyone is a lot less likely to really listen to what's being said.

Listening is also a lot more effective if you sit down without distractions, so put down your screens and focus fully on the people around you. Ask everyone to talk in turn about screen use, and let each person speak without interrupting.

Try these four prompts if you need to encourage anyone to start talking:

What do you do when you go online?

Whom do you talk to online?

What aspect of your screen use bothers you?

What aspect of anyone else's use of screens bothers you?

Don't expect to solve all of your family issues around screens with just one session. This is a big subject and talking about it is an ongoing activity for everyone in the family, especially as any children will be moving through different stages in their screen use as they grow up. But regular sessions where you talk and really listen will mean you'll avoid the arguments that come when you haven't tried to understand each other.

"Organize an active listening session to kick off talking about screens at home."

2

MODELING

Whenever I talk to children and young people about their screen use I can guarantee there will be at least one hand raised at the end of my talk: "I can easily put down social media, but my parents are always glued to it."

So many of our worries about screen overuse seem focused on children, and yet how many important family conversations and moments are parents missing out on because they are looking at their smartphone, tablet, or laptop?

Adults in any family home are used to modeling the behavior they expect from their children. From good manners to healthy eating, parents show their children by their own behavior what's expected in their family. Screen time must be part of this too. If we have a screen device glued to our hands while telling others to put their tablets and games consoles down, we're going to be met with increased resistance.

The first step to modeling good screen habits is self-awareness. Try keeping a diary to record your screen use at home for a week to help you get a better understanding of what others around you are seeing. For each day, note down the amount of time you've spent on each different type of screen activity, and remember to be honest.

Once you've built up a picture of your own screen use, assess where you can cut down. Make a conscious effort to model the screen behavior you want to encourage in younger people in your house. Some ideas could be:

When talking to anyone at home, put your phone away, completely out of sight, and fully focus on them.

Don't pick up your phone in the morning until everyone has gone off to school, college, or work.

Abide by any unique rules on screen use you've set for your family.

Older siblings should also be aware that any younger children in their family notice and copy their behavior too. All of us, at any age, need to realize that our habits don't go unnoticed: we're living in close proximity with people who pick up on our every move.

See how much easier it is to talk about screens when everyone is following the same rules, and how many really productive conversations open up as a result.

"Make a conscious effort to model the screen behavior you want to encourage in younger people in your house."

3

TABOOS

The online world is vast and, like any other area of life, there are dark corners and shadowy behaviors that we might rather ignore and pretend aren't there. But talking about screen use inevitably involves recognizing that some content and behavior online is unpleasant, unsettling, and can be dangerous.

Schools everywhere are educating children about dangers online but, for the rest of us, the temptation is to ignore these aspects of screen life until they *have* to be acknowledged and confronted. With everyone increasingly absorbed in their digital lives, we all need to learn how to deal with something we may encounter online that is upsetting or disturbing, and help others too.

In your discussions about screen use in the home, try this question as a conversation starter:

Have you ever seen anything online that has upset or bothered you?

It can also be productive if you phrase it as a question about someone else:

Do any of your friends get involved in risky behavior online? or
Have any of your friends come across anything upsetting online?

These questions are a more neutral way to encourage a younger child to open up and disclose something that's troubling them without fear of getting into trouble.

As well as content posted by others, there is also the issue of content that family members create or share themselves. With the explosion in picture messaging, we are all now creating a huge amount of unique content and uploading and sharing it daily. One useful way to get everyone to think about the visibility of content they create is the "T-shirt test."

In one of your chats at home about screen life, suggest that next time anyone is about to post or share something online they think about wearing it on a T-shirt. Ask everyone to report back on whether it changed their behavior, whether they decided not to post something, or modified it in any way. You don't need to ask anyone to disclose *what* material he or she was thinking of for this to be very effective.

Make the T-shirt test a handy piece of family shorthand for discussing appropriate behavior online.

4

ECHO CHAMBERS

When you ask everyone at home what they do when they go online, social media is bound to be one of the biggest areas of their online activity. Following people on social media who have similar interests and views to us is one of the joys of our digital lives, and it can be particularly helpful in the teenage years when children are finding their identities.

But one of the dangers of following people who are similar to ourselves is that we can ignore a huge part of the world that has a different experience of life. Social media apps exacerbate this narrowing of our perspectives when they suggest people to follow based on similarities we have with those who are already in our online network. This can lead to us being in an "echo chamber" online—when our opinions get reflected back to us with no disagreement. It can feel great, but it might not help us understand different views.

The great gift of the internet is that we now have access to a huge amount of information. We can learn about different countries, cultures, and opinions much more easily than when we lived in quite small and homogenous communities before the digital age.

We can also connect with people all over the world and get a glimpse into their lives. When I give talks about the online world in schools, one of the things I encourage young people to do (and this is just as valid for adults) is to seek out people online who are completely different from them. People from different countries; people whose backgrounds and life experiences are utterly different from their own.

Suggest to everyone at home that they broaden their online horizons this week and share with everyone else what they have learned. You could follow someone from a different country, for example, or research two sides of a debate that's in the news.

I guarantee you will all learn something new and expand your perspectives.

CHAPTER

2

TAKING
CONTROL

When your phone is on the table during a family meal or furtively glanced at when you're talking to someone, the message you're sending to those you live with is "This device is more important to me than you." Notice how it makes you feel when other people are doing this to you. Adults and children may rail against each other's screen habits, but we can all be guilty of unwittingly prioritizing our screens over spending time with our loved ones. How do we put screens back in their place?

Taking control of our devices, instead of allowing them to control us, is difficult. It's inevitable that bad screen habits are easy to slip into. Smartphones, tablets, games consoles, and the software that runs on them are designed to be "sticky," hard to ignore, and yes, addictive. Digital designers study the ways our brains work and create features in their technology that give us surges of dopamine—the "feel-good chemical."

Whether we're playing on a games console or scrolling on a smartphone hoping for a text or a "like" on something we've posted on social media, our brains are waiting for tiny dopamine hits. As our dopamine levels rise, our brains respond by wanting more. And this can start to affect our family life—when screen time encroaches on sleep hours and irritability and tiredness cause rows, or when mealtimes are a missed opportunity to reconnect because everyone is scrolling.

But lessening the hold that screens have over you is simple if you try a few techniques that I have used for a number of years now to help people reduce their time on screens. Being aware of the messages we are sending when we can't put our screens down is the first step. Deciding to take control of our device use is the next. This section will give you ideas for different ways of taking control.

HAVE YOU SET CLEAR
BOUNDARIES FOR SCREEN
USE AT HOME?

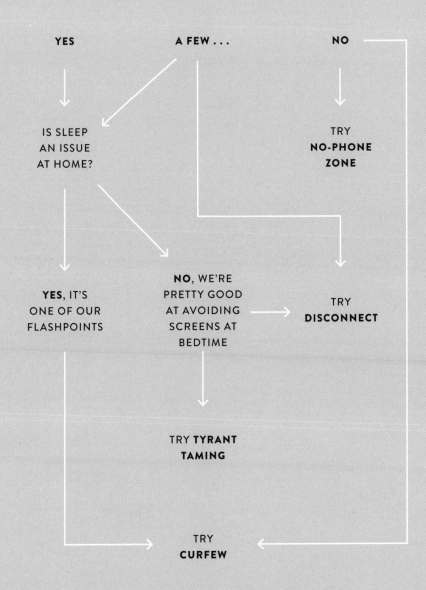

YES   A FEW . . .   NO

IS SLEEP
AN ISSUE
AT HOME?

TRY
**NO-PHONE
ZONE**

YES, IT'S
ONE OF OUR
FLASHPOINTS

NO, WE'RE
PRETTY GOOD
AT AVOIDING
SCREENS AT
BEDTIME

TRY
DISCONNECT

TRY **TYRANT
TAMING**

TRY
CURFEW

1

CURFEW

When we're tired at home petty irritations and disagreements have a tendency of spiraling out of control. Making sure everyone gets a good night's sleep is one of the foundations of a happy home life. Unfortunately, good sleep is more and more the casualty of our screen-based lives. Everywhere you look adults and young people seem to be yawning and complaining that they're not getting enough sleep.

The blue light that shines from our screen-based devices is the guilty party in a large part of our sleep deprivation. That light, designed to mimic daylight and make us more engaged with our screens, interferes with the production of melatonin (the "sleep" hormone) and can leave us feeling wide awake and alert, just at the time we need to wind down. One study recently showed that teenagers who spend more than four hours per day on screens were 3.5 times more likely to get poor sleep (sleeping fewer than five hours at night) than those who spent under four hours on screens per day.

Experiment in your own home with different approaches to sleep and screens, and give some, or all, of the following ideas a go.

CAN'T RELAX?

If you live with someone who's always looking at their phone in the evening you'll probably have noticed that they find it hard to wind down. Agree a cut-off time for tech use, and get everyone in the family relearning screen-free alternatives for relaxing in the evening, such as reading a book or having a hot, non-caffeinated drink.

LOSING SLEEP?

You don't even need to be using screens right up until bedtime for your screen use to be interfering with your sleep. Limiting the number of total hours you spend on screens each day and putting your devices down at regular points will make switching off at night that much easier.

PERMANENTLY ATTACHED?

Many of us keep our phones on our bedside table, next to us while we sleep. That means we often reach for them automatically before we go to bed or if we wake up during the night. Set a time when all screens have to be outside the bedroom door so there's a reduced temptation to look at them. You could also set up a charging station in a central place in the house, to keep phones out of bedrooms at night.

"Making sure everyone
gets a good night's sleep
is one of the foundations
of a happy home life."

2

TYRANT TAMING

If you live with anyone who has every last notification enabled on their smartphone you'll know that the barrage of dings, beeps, and pop-ups flashing on their screen can be quite overwhelming. Conversations constantly interrupted by messaging app alerts on multiple devices can be a flashpoint of home life.

Of course, software companies design notifications to be hard to ignore—that's what makes their technology successful. But with approximately one hundred apps installed on the average smartphone, we're all in danger of being in thrall to the tyrants in our pockets, picking them up and putting them down endlessly and having them constantly interrupting our train of thought, and our conversations, even if we don't respond instantly to their alerts.

Most of our digital devices have in-built customizable features that we can use to reduce interruptions, but many of us don't explore them. And there are lots of low-tech ways to cut down on screen distractions. Suggest that everyone at home tries all or some of the following ideas.

CAN YOU SEE IT?

Is your device face-up on the table so you can always see when a new notification pops up? If our phones are visible, we're immediately more distracted, always waiting for a new alert. Just the sight of a phone, even when it's not making a noise, can increase anxiety. If you're not using your phone, put it away so it's out of sight.

CAN YOU HEAR IT?

Even if you have a rule at home that devices should be put away when everyone is together, the sound of gadgets pinging or vibrating can be very hard to ignore. Start by suggesting you turn off all sounds when you're together as family. Better still, turn off your screens altogether.

CAN YOU FEEL IT?

Is your phone always in the pocket nearest your body so you can reflexively pat it from time to time? Trying to ignore your phone when it's physically the closest thing to you is difficult. An effective solution is a drawer that everyone puts their devices in during family time. So simple, but it really works.

3

NO-PHONE ZONE

Arguing about devices at mealtimes is surely a feature of most family homes today. Even if you've agreed in principle that they don't belong there, screens have a tendency to creep back in when someone is "waiting for an urgent email" or "needing to send a message about meeting up later." Tempers get frayed when those who are abiding by the rules watch others break them.

In your conversations about screen use at home, start by agreeing where and when screens don't belong. It's a thorny subject and you will all have very different views about where your family "no-phone zones" should be, but it's important you work it out together and come to some agreement. Decide which areas you will make screen-free so you can focus on each other, or where you will spend time alone on pursuits offscreen. Here are a few ideas to discuss.

MAPPING THE HOUSE

Sit everyone down and sketch out a map of the house together to agree your family no-go zones for devices. Screens definitely don't belong in the bedrooms of younger members of the family. But how about making that the rule for adults at home, too? And how many of us can honestly say we never take our devices into the bathroom? Consider marking bedrooms and bathrooms with an "X" on your map.

THE KITCHEN OR DINING ROOM

A strong family life revolves around the conversations we have at mealtimes. Meals are the main times when we can all get together and check in with each other about our day ahead or the day just ending. Sitting in silence and scrolling through your devices is not a good way to strengthen your connection. If you haven't already banned screens in the kitchen or dining room, then this is a good place to start.

THE CAR

Tempting though it is to let everyone scroll on their devices during car journeys for the sake of a bit of peace, how about making the car a place where you all talk to each other, listen to music together, or even play a game? Sometimes the most valuable conversations between parents and children, or between partners, can happen in the car. Let's not lose all those opportunities.

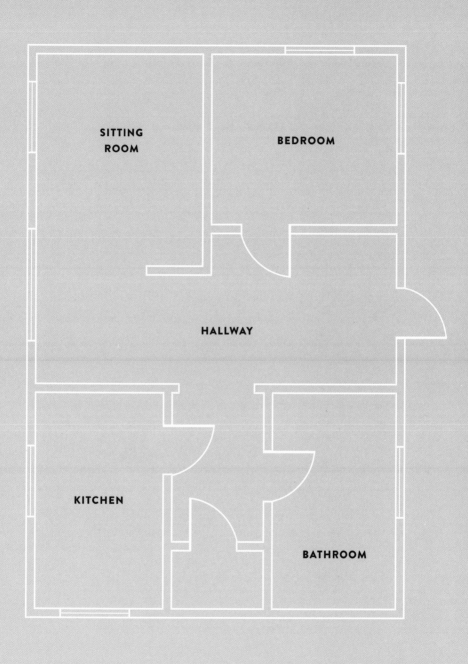

SITTING ROOM

BEDROOM

HALLWAY

KITCHEN

BATHROOM

4

DISCONNECT

It used to be that if there was a problem at school, coming home at the end of the day meant a night cooling off to diffuse any tensions. Similarly, the pressures of work life used to end at the office door. But the 24/7 connection that social media, messaging, and emails give us via our smartphones and tablets means that problems now follow us home and into our downtime, and we never really get the chance to switch off and take a break from what's worrying us.

To give everyone in the home a taste of what disconnecting properly once in a while might do for them, plan some completely screen-free home time. With practice, it will start to feel more natural and become just another aspect of your life at home.

SET A DATE	Discuss with everyone when the best time to go screen-free would be so that anxieties about not being contactable don't interfere.
STICK TO THE RULES	Find a safe place to store everyone's screens so they are completely out of sight.
AGREE A TIME LIMIT	Start with just a few screen-free hours the first time you try, and build up to longer and longer periods. Your first mini goal might be a screen-free weekend. Longer-term, challenge yourselves to have a holiday together completely off-line.
PLAN SCREEN-FREE ALTERNATIVES	Give yourself a good chance of success by deciding what you're going to do to occupy your screen-free hours. You could do something very practical, such as giving cupboards a good clear out, or it might be a good opportunity to go for a walk or a bike ride. You'll find more ideas for activities to try in your screen-free time in Chapter 7.

CHAPTER

FINDING
BALANCE

We can quite easily recognize when someone we live with isn't eating healthily. If a member of our family is snacking on junk food, not eating enough fruit and vegetables, and then complaining about being out of shape, we might gently suggest a different approach to food. But do we notice, and talk about, whether our digital diets are healthy?

Part of the problem is that because the digital world is so new, there's very little consensus on what "healthy" looks like for screen use. Some researchers think that measuring the amount of *time* is important: in that way of thinking we'd set a daily limit of screen minutes. Others think that what we *do* on screens is more important. With that approach we'd think of balanced screen time like a balanced diet, and we might monitor scrolling without purpose against using screens for something productive. With conflicting approaches, how can we decide what works best for us at home?

One suggestion is to focus on the *results* of our screen habits. If we notice that someone at home is not sleeping and they're *also* spending many hours on screens, that could be a time to talk about whether the two might be connected. Similarly, if we notice that someone we live with is in a persistently low mood and they're also spending a lot of their screen time on social media, we'd probably want to talk about the effect the online world is having on them.

To decide what your family digital diet should look like, you first need to assess whether you're all thriving. If everyone at home feels well and happy, you're probably all using screens in a way that's healthy. If there are areas of concern, you might want to consider your family digital consumption and experiment with what "healthy" looks like for all of you. In this section there are some ideas for doing just that.

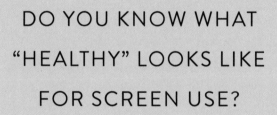

DO YOU KNOW WHAT
"HEALTHY" LOOKS LIKE
FOR SCREEN USE?

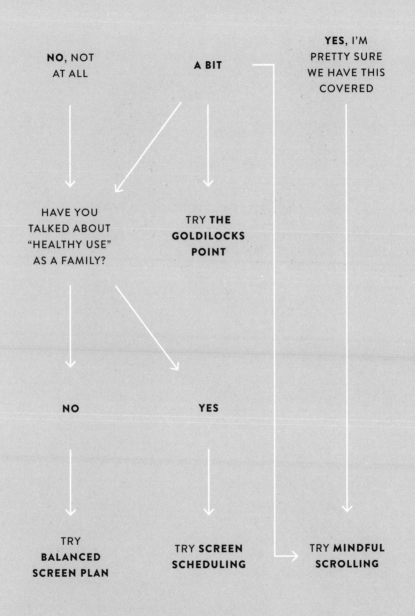

NO, NOT
AT ALL

A BIT

YES, I'M
PRETTY SURE
WE HAVE THIS
COVERED

HAVE YOU
TALKED ABOUT
"HEALTHY USE"
AS A FAMILY?

TRY **THE
GOLDILOCKS
POINT**

NO

YES

TRY
**BALANCED
SCREEN PLAN**

TRY **SCREEN
SCHEDULING**

TRY **MINDFUL
SCROLLING**

1

BALANCED SCREEN PLAN

There are many different ways of using screens. There might be someone at home who is heavily into gaming but hardly ever picks up their phone. Someone else may use their screens mainly for social media; you yourself may spend hours looking at emails and messages.

We've probably had to agree basic ground rules for what food we all eat together to avoid complete chaos at mealtimes. How do we agree ground rules for our family digital diet? Use this exercise to help you think about your screen use like nutrition and set some healthy guidelines.

THE SCREEN-USE PLATE

1. Draw a large circle, about the size of a dinner plate, on a piece of paper.
2. Make a list on a second piece of paper of all the different ways you and your family use screens. Split these into work, play, and junk. Activities that come under these three areas could be:

WORK—sending and responding to emails, using information and resource sites online for work and education projects

PLAY—connecting with family and friends on social media, playing computer games, watching videos, sharing memes

JUNK—being online for no particular reason, reaching for screens when bored, picking up screens out of habit and for distraction

3. Talk about what a "healthy" screen plate might look like for your family at home. How much screen time at home should be for work and how much for play? Focus on that "junk" segment, too—do you all agree that it should be cut down to allow more focus on the other two areas?

4. Draw the three types of screen use proportionally on your "plate," like a pie chart. Then try to translate your intentions into guidelines (for example, "we each have 30 minutes at home per day for spending time on social media.") Mark minutes or hours and any explanations in each area.

5. Stick your family screen plate on the fridge and be prepared to debate and adjust its pattern for a while until you reach a balance that feels right.

"Talk about what
  a 'healthy' screen plate
  might look like for
  your family at home."

2

MINDFUL SCROLLING

Whether it's children claiming that they're only using a screen for an essential school project, or parents protesting that they're picking up their smartphone again for "work," we all pretend to ourselves that what we're using our screens for is constructive and essential.

But how many times do we notice ourselves and each other spending more time on our screens than we said we would? Persuasive technology is designed to distract and lure us into spending more time online than we originally intended. Videos that immediately start auto-playing after the ones we've just watched, suggestions for new content to read, or new people to follow on social media—these can all seduce us into scrolling online for hours without any real purpose.

To avoid this type of time-wasting on screens we need to be mindful, not mindless, when we use our devices.

1. Set an intention for your screen time. Is it to check your emails, research a project, or send a message to a friend?

2. Mentally set a time limit for how long you think this activity will take you.

3. Carry out your intended task. Keep an eye on the time and notice if you've over- or underestimated the time you thought it would take you.

4. Put down your screen when you've accomplished your task.

Notice how easy or hard you find this. Did you spend a longer time on your screen than you intended because other things online distracted you? Don't be hard on yourself if this is the case to start with. Just keep practicing the skill of going online with a purpose. And share with each other at home any tips or tricks you find to make it easier.

"We need to be mindful,
not mindless, when
we use our devices."

3

THE "GOLDILOCKS" POINT

"You've been on that thing for *too long*!" Have you heard that shout in your home recently? But how much is "too long?" As our screen lives are so new there hasn't yet been much research on the subject. But one Oxford and Cardiff University study looked at outcomes for teenagers and found that spending roughly four hours per day on screens had a positive effect on their well-being. It's been called the "Goldilocks" point— and it's reached when the amount of time spent on screens is just right.

At up to four hours per day on screens the teenagers were better off than those who spent zero hours per day—so banning screens altogether is not a good idea. But spending more than four hours on screens per day caused the teenagers' well-being to suffer. We don't have similar research for adults or much younger children, but the Goldilocks point is a good place to start. How can you make this work for your family?

It might help to know that the just-right point differed depending on the type of screen used, as you can see opposite (but it didn't take into account whether screens were used for schoolwork or play: all on-screen activity was considered equal).

Playing video games: 1 hour 40 minutes
Using a smartphone: 1 hour 57 minutes
Watching TV and films: 3 hours 41 minutes
Using computers: 4 hours 17 minutes

Set your own Goldilocks points for everyone's just-right daily screen use. Think of it a bit like bedtimes, with limits changing as children get older and adapting for changes in term and holiday time. Remember this study was for teenagers, so for younger people at home you ought to be thinking well below the four-hours point.

4

SCREEN SCHEDULING

How many times have we avoided confrontation or difficult conversations with someone at home by burying our heads in a screen? Partners can be just as guilty of doing this to each other as children and parents are.

But there are some points during the day when we really need to reconnect with each other to strengthen our relationships, and we simply can't do that if we're on our screens. As part of your agreement for screen time at home, set some sacrosanct time slots, and agree to avoid using screens for distraction or avoidance. Some ideas might be:

SCREEN-FREE MORNINGS

Before you all leave the house in the morning, carve out some screen-free time to allow you to focus on each other. Put all screens away and talk about your intentions for the day. Leave the house feeling buoyed up by each other's attention and support.

STRAIGHT IN THE DOOR

When you all come in from work or school, it's the perfect time to check in and share how your day went, unload any frustrations or problems, and celebrate each other's successes. Try thinking of the doorway of your home as an airport scanner that will alert you to the presence of your phone on your body. As you walk through the door, put your screens down in a central place so you can focus on each other.

GOLDEN HOUR

Bath and bedtimes can be really special times for a family, especially if there are younger children in the home. Being on a smartphone while you're supervising a bath or giving a child a tablet to play on (instead of reading a book together) diminishes the power of those moments. Agree that bath, story, and bedtimes should be screen-free and make the most of times that won't last forever.

CHAPTER

HEALTHY
BODIES

Playing on a games console in a bedroom, working on a laptop in the kitchen, scrolling on a smartphone while watching TV—all of these activities involve us being mostly sedentary and in a bent-over posture looking down at a screen. If we look around our homes tonight we can probably see members of our family in that distinctive hunch as they peer downward at their devices.

When we talk about the impact screens might be having on us, many of our conversations are about the effects on our mental health. But with our devices now being our constant companions at home and work, the fact is that they are affecting us physically too.

We now know how to design classrooms and office workstations so that they are ergonomic, and that means most of us are pretty good at looking after our bodies when we're on screens in our places of work or at school. But we haven't given much thought to the physical-health aspects of using screens in our family homes. It's no good using screens in a way that's healthy outside the home if we come in and simply ignore all those important messages about posture, lighting, or screen placement.

Maybe you've noticed someone at home complaining about physical aches and pains? Perhaps they have a persistenly sore or stiff neck or are always rubbing what look like very sore eyes? If those same people are the ones you most often see hunched over their screens, then there's a good chance their symptoms may be caused (or at least exacerbated) by their screen use.

In this section there are some suggestions of physical symptoms to look out for in each other that might be caused by unhealthy screen habits, and ideas on how to counter them.

ARE YOU ALL

FIGHTING FIT?

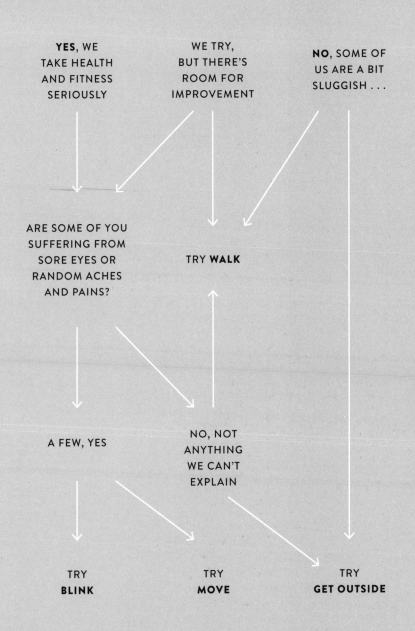

YES, WE TAKE HEALTH AND FITNESS SERIOUSLY

WE TRY, BUT THERE'S ROOM FOR IMPROVEMENT

NO, SOME OF US ARE A BIT SLUGGISH . . .

ARE SOME OF YOU SUFFERING FROM SORE EYES OR RANDOM ACHES AND PAINS?

TRY **WALK**

A FEW, YES

NO, NOT ANYTHING WE CAN'T EXPLAIN

TRY **BLINK**

TRY **MOVE**

TRY **GET OUTSIDE**

1

BLINK

Have you noticed anyone at home rubbing their eyes a lot lately, and not at a time of day when it could be reasonably blamed on tiredness? Is anyone in the family complaining of dry or sore eyes, or getting headaches more frequently?

If you're noticing these symptoms in yourself and others at home, you might be affected by "digital eyestrain." Eye doctors are reporting more and more cases of this condition, particularly in young people, and it's caused by focusing on harsh light-emitting screens for too long and not blinking frequently enough. Here are three different exercises you can all use to help your eyes while using screens.

20-20-20

Every 20 minutes, look away from your screen and focus on an object at least 20 feet away, for at least 20 seconds. Looking at an object in the distance relaxes the focusing muscle inside your eye.

SHUT-EYE

Every 20 minutes, blink 10 times by closing your eyes very slowly, as if you were falling asleep. When looking at a screen we blink much less frequently (about one third as often as normal), and a lot of the blinking we do isn't fully closing our eyes, according to studies. Blinking very deliberately and fully like this re-wets our eyes and reduces dryness and irritation.

NEAR AND FAR

Look far away at a distant object (at least 20 feet away) for 10–15 seconds, and then switch your gaze to something up close (under six inches away) for 10–15 seconds. Switch between the near and far object 10 times, focusing your gaze each time for 10–15 seconds. "Focusing fatigue" is one of the causes of digital eyestrain, and this exercise reduces the risk of your eyes' focusing ability "locking up" after prolonged screen time.

"Look far away at a distant object . . . and then switch your gaze to something up close."

2

MOVE

Hunching over screens, like we might do on our smartphones at home on the sofa, is one of the worst things we can do for our spines. The average human head weighs about 10 pounds, but for every inch we tilt our heads forward, the pressure on our spine doubles. So if we're looking down at a smartphone at chest or waist height our necks are holding up what feels like 20 pounds to our spines. Of course, our spines are able to take increases in pressure when we look down, but not for hours at a time every day.

Try these three exercises when family necks and shoulders are aching and painful and you all feel like they might be taking the strain from screen overuse.

COBRA

Lie facedown on the floor with your legs stretched out and your hands directly under your shoulders. Raise your head, tuck your chin in and look down at the floor while taking your hands off the floor and squeezing your shoulder blades together. Raise your legs off the floor at the same time. Return to lying down. Repeat 10 times.

CHICKEN

Sit on a chair with both feet flat on the floor and look straight ahead. Slowly move your head backward while keeping your chin tucked in and down. Keep looking straight ahead and don't tilt your face upward. When you've reached as far as feels comfortable, hold this position for about 10 seconds. Then relax, and your head and neck should automatically move forward to your starting position. Repeat five times.

EAR TO SHOULDER

Again, sit on a chair with your feet flat on the floor. Extend your left hand up and place it on the crown of your head, near the right. Point your elbow out to the side. Gently pull your head to the left, directing your left ear to your left shoulder. Hold for 20 seconds. Switch sides and use your right hand to pull your head gently toward your right shoulder. Do this as many times as feels comfortable to relax your neck muscles.

3

WALK

When we come in from work, school, or college at the end
of each day, the first thing many of us do is sit down. But the
majority of us have been been sitting down for most of the
day, too. Moving our bodies when we've been sedentary for so
long is a good antidote to both the physical and mental effects
of screen overuse.

Walking is an easy way to incorporate physical activity into
our day, and it's also one of the best things we can do to take
care of ourselves. Talk as a family about how you can build
some more walking into your daily lives. Some starting points
could be:

SWAP TYRES FOR FEET

Can any aspects of your daily journeys, usually carried out on
buses, trains, or cars, be swapped for walking? You could walk
the school run one day a week, for example, or walk one section
of a work commute.

WALKING CHORES

Even a relatively mundane task like posting a letter or picking up a few groceries becomes something to enjoy and savor when you do it on foot instead of in a car. Find something small you need to collect or deliver and set out on a walking expedition together.

EVENING STROLL

Try going for a walk straight after work or school, before you all sit down to do homework, or cook the evening meal, or slump in front of the television. Even a quick 20-minute walk will invigorate and refresh you.

"Talk as a family about how you can build some walking into your daily lives."

4

GET OUTSIDE

Going outside gives us a chance to take a break from our screens and leave our devices behind. Keep an eye on each other's device use and encourage everyone to get off screens and go outside at regular intervals. Adopt this as a family rule, posted somewhere prominent to remind you all:

FIFTEEN MINUTES OF FRESH AIR FOR EVERY HOUR SPENT ON SCREENS.

Act as each other's coaches and encourage everyone to take a break when screen use seems to be going on too long. Better still, take your fresh-air breaks together. Throw a ball or frisbee around a green space, run a much-needed errand, or walk the dog as a family.

If you're doing something time-sensitive for work or school and can't take a long break, simply opening the front door, going outside, and standing in the fresh air looking up at the sky for a few minutes will get you off your screen and clear your head. Making the effort to reconnect with the world outside may even encourage you to then walk around the block for five minutes.

It's particularly hard when it's cold or raining to make yourself step outside, but when you do you'll come back to your screen rested and more productive than if you sit in front of it for hours.

CHAPTER

5

HEALTHY MINDS

Laughter, fun, and familiarity bind us together as families. We often have our own insider jokes that no one else quite understands—and we know exactly which aspects of our behavior can annoy other people in our family, too.

So it's obvious to us when someone at home is withdrawing from family interactions and is not as happy as they might be. Our relationship with our screens can play a part in this. Being constantly available and having our devices constantly at hand leaves us more stressed, anxious, and at higher risk of burnout.

Excessive time spent on social media in particular can have an insidious effect on our self-confidence and self-esteem. Of course, we know we all curate our own social media feeds carefully: we only show the best angle, the most flattering light, and the most exhilarating holiday experience. Yet we tend to forget that when we are looking at other people's posts. There's no substitute for building self-esteem off-line.

CHAPTER 5

When a teenager is disappearing into their room to play computer games deep into the night, missing out on sleep; when another is spending hours online and becoming increasingly self-critical; when a partner comes home from the office and is visibly stressed from a constant stream of work emails around the clock: these are clues that our relationship with screens may be taking a toll on our mental health.

If our time on devices is making us feel irritable or depressed, or disconnected from others at home, it's definitely a sign that something is awry. For most of us though, the issue is just that we've got things a bit out of balance, with too much time spent online and not enough time spent off screens, relaxing and recharging.

In this section, each exercise is designed to look at aspects of mental health that might be negatively affected by excess screen time and gently bolster self-esteem, build confidence, and boost happiness.

IS EVERYONE

HAPPY AT HOME?

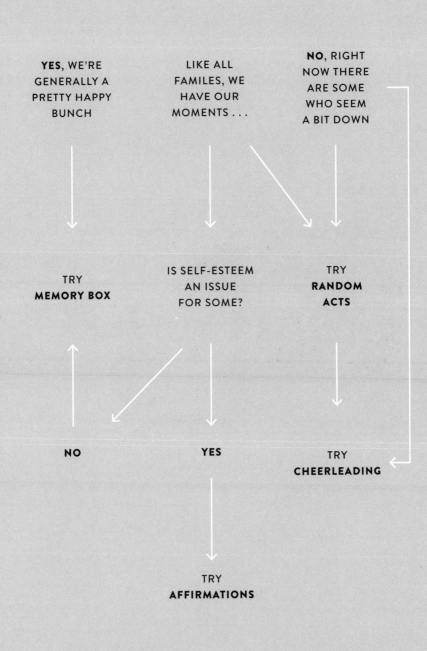

1

RANDOM ACTS

One of the best ways to start feeling better about yourself is to think about, and do something for, others. Think about all the different ways your family has shown kindness to you: a parent driving you somewhere because you're late, your partner giving you flowers after a bad day. These are the little gestures of love that bond you as a family and offer an essential assurance: you care and you have each other's backs.

Choose a random act of kindness to perform for a sibling, partner, parent, or child today. Here are some ideas to get you started.

ASK A FAMILY MEMBER ABOUT THEIR DAY

Instead of settling for "fine" or "ok," probe a little deeper and you may find that something is troubling them, or that they are really excited about something and want to share it. Small gestures like eye contact, a hug, or a smile also make a big difference, and they're all things we don't get with online communication.

CLEAN A COMMON AREA

It's so easy for a busy family home to start to resemble a disaster area, but a tidy environment can be an essential refuge. When our heads are cluttered and busy, it's relaxing and reassuring to find order elsewhere. Tackle an area that everyone uses, enjoy a sense of achievement, and be surprised by the appreciation you receive.

A SURPRISE MEAL

If you don't normally cook, give the person who does a break and create a special occasion by serving up a family treat. Cook a dish you all know and love, or make something inspired by the cuisine of a place you once visited together.

Be creative and think about as many different ideas as possible. It might help to step into the shoes of the person you want to surprise to figure out what really might help.

"Cook a dish you all know and love."

2

CHEERLEADING

Isn't it true that we often seem far more appreciative of those outside our families than the people we live with, whom we comfortably take for granted? Adults and children at home may use very different social media platforms and online communities, but we all act in a similar way: we tell others that we like what they've posted, we love their selfies, we appreciate their talents, and support them in their struggles.

When was the last time you did this for someone you live with? Is there someone in your home right now who needs a bit of cheerleading from you, to let him or her know you appreciate them?

Social media makes it easy to show appreciation: we can like or share someone's post with just a click of a mouse. But cheering someone on off-line can be a thousand times more meaningful and lasting.

Write a letter of appreciation to someone in your family for a birthday present, to cheer them up, or for no reason at all other than to show you care.

1. Write the letter by hand, don't type it: that extra bit of effort will be noticed.

2. Think about what you really appreciate about this family member. Is it their support of you? How hard they work for you all? The way they always have your back? Their groan-worthy jokes that make you laugh after a bad day?

3. Try to recall a particular incident—praise and feedback is always much more powerful if it's specific—and let the person know how they helped or encouraged you, or buoyed you up.

4. Put the letter in an envelope and leave it in a place they will find it, or give it to them personally if it's for a special occasion.

Don't be surprised if your letter becomes a much-treasured item that means a very great deal to the recipient—something to be taken out and read and reread at times when they need a bit of a boost.

"Cheering someone on off-line can be a thousand times more meaningful and lasting."

3

MEMORY BOX

So many important family memories are now stored solely in cyberspace, posted on "walls," or left languishing on smartphone camera rolls. It used to be that a family photo album took pride of place in every home: a huge heavy object, it was something every family could sit down and pore over together. Due our hectic lifestyles and the time it takes to put photo albums together, it's just become easier to post and keep everything online. But this means we've lost those times when we can relive our happy memories and achievements as a family.

To make storing and enjoying family memories as simple and quick as posting online, find an oversized container that will be your family "memory box." Throw in any physical items that will remind you of experiences you've enjoyed together as a couple or family. Ideas might be:

Tickets and festival wristbands
Art projects
Sports caps, certificates, and medals
Birthday cards
Photos

Encourage everyone in the family to see the box as "theirs," to add items to that have any particular significance for them, as and when they want. Don't let any editing happen—just throw in any items you wish (over time you may need more than one box).

Find a time to sit down together, pick out objects at random, and talk about what you remember and enjoyed—it could be at Christmas or New Year, or during a rainy weekend. Let going through the memory box be something that creates a few more happy family memories of its own.

4

APHORISMS

AND AFFIRMATIONS

The online world is peppered with memes and motivational quotes, and if you ask anyone at home if they've seen or shared any good ones recently, I'm sure you can all come up with a few. You may not know that appreciating the power of affirmations didn't just arise with the birth of the digital world. Leonardo da Vinci was a big fan of writing affirmations daily to encourage him to continue working. "I do not depart from my furrow" and "Obstacles do not bend me" are just two he wrote in his notebook to spur himself on.

Affirmations and aphorisms are short and simple positive statements about yourself and your actions that you repeat until you start to believe them. You're really just training your brain to think positively about yourself and to focus on the behavior and result you want by gentle repetition. Use this exercise to create some affirmations for your family home.

1. Gather together scissors, card, paper, old magazines, and colored crayons and pens.

2. Think about something that's important to you and the outcome you want. Frame it positively— your affirmation should reflect what you want to happen, not what you *don't* want to happen, for example: "I'm a mathematics wizard!", not "I won't fail my exam."

3. Design your affirmation card or poster in the most colorful and exciting way possible. Go mad and use cut-out pictures, drawings, neon-bright writing— anything to make it look really enticing, inspiring, and eye-catching.

4. Stick your affirmation somewhere where you will see it every day—on a mirror in your bedroom, or propped up on your desk or bedside table.

5. Discuss creating family affirmations for everyone, such as "We take care of our bodies every day" to inspire you all. Put these in family spaces so you can all see them.

CHAPTER

6

WORK

Home sets the tone for our day and affects our productivity, and excess time spent on screens here has a direct effect on how well we perform at work, school, or college.

The essential part technology plays in our lives and its ability to present multiple windows simultaneously encourages a culture of multi-tasking, speedy solutions, and instantaneous responses. If you're trying to revise for an exam but keeping one eye on social media, or writing a report on a laptop while checking your emails on a smartphone, you're trying to multitask. But by doing this, are we really getting more done? An attempt to multitask simply splits our focus across several different things, limiting our effectiveness at any of them.

You don't even need to be juggling between activities to lose focus. Studies have shown that merely having a mobile phone in the same room as you when you are trying to focus (even if you don't look at it) can distract you and stop you from concentrating properly.

Screen use may also be changing how our brains actually function, affecting how well we do our work. At the more extreme end of the scale, brain scans of those with serious internet or gaming addictions show deterioration in areas of the brain that affect planning, prioritizing, and problem-solving.

All of this may sound worrying. And there's no doubt that if you have a serious problem with screens you might notice some of these things. However, most of us can find easy ways to prevent these negative effects, one being to log off regularly. In this section you'll find ideas that will help you refresh and restore mental abilities that might need a bit of sharpening up after too much time spent on screens.

IS YOUR WORK

GOING WELL?

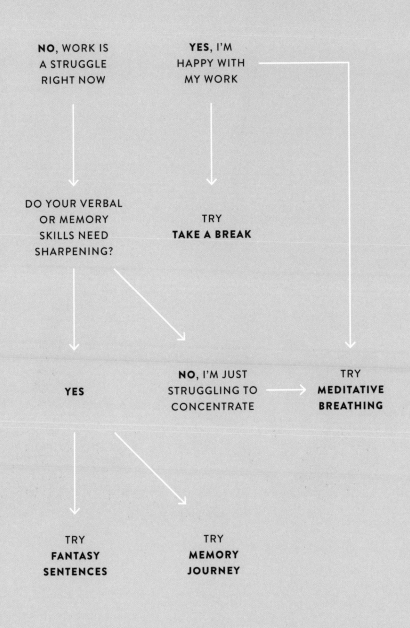

NO, WORK IS
A STRUGGLE
RIGHT NOW

YES, I'M
HAPPY WITH
MY WORK

DO YOUR VERBAL
OR MEMORY
SKILLS NEED
SHARPENING?

TRY
TAKE A BREAK

YES

NO, I'M JUST
STRUGGLING TO
CONCENTRATE

TRY
**MEDITATIVE
BREATHING**

TRY
**FANTASY
SENTENCES**

TRY
**MEMORY
JOURNEY**

1

MEDITATIVE BREATHING

At home, at work, and at school, our devices are constantly buzzing and our minds are buzzing too. We are overloaded with information and struggling to say "no," "stop," or "enough." Constantly available, our brains can quickly feel frazzled, our focus nonexistent, and our tempers short at the escalating demands on our attention.

Anyone who has seen a child who has spent several hours on a computer or a parent playing email tennis on a smartphone will have witnessed that "wired" and distracted air about them. That's the very opposite of what we need at home to reduce anxiety and stress.

One way to combat screen stimulation and find focus is to practice meditative breathing.

1. **START BY SITTING WITH BOTH FEET FLAT ON THE GROUND.** Rest your hands gently in your lap, with your palms facing up or nestled one inside the other.

2. **FOCUS ON THE PATTERN OF YOUR BREATHING.** Notice the individual breaths, in and out.

3. **COUNT UP TO 10 BREATHS.** Once you have finished the first set, begin again at one. Keep counting in sets of 10 breaths. Alternatively, try repeating "in, out" silently in your head as you breathe.

If you notice that your mind has wandered off course and thoughts pop into your head, gently bring your attention back to your breathing. Try not to get frustrated or annoyed when this happens—it's simply inevitable. When you do get distracted, take care to acknowledge it, and bring your attention back to your breathing. Remember to be kind to yourself, and be patient.

Build up to being able to do this exercise for 20 minutes at a time. With regular practice you will start to see improvements in your focus and concentration.

For the next step up, use this technique to help you "single-task." Try focusing one activity, such as reading a book or writing a school assignment, giving it your full and undivided attention. Each time you feel your mind wandering and you get the urge to check your phone or emails, use this breathing technique to block out distractions and help you focus.

"With regular practice you will start to see improvements in your focus and concentration."

2

MEMORY JOURNEY

We all use calculators, together with a variety of apps, to do some of the heavy lifting our brains used to do. These tools are one of the huge advantages of the digital world, but when we become too reliant on them we allow valuable parts of our mental abilities to get rusty with lack of use. We can combat this by switching back to analogue alternatives, such as using mental arithmetic to do any calculations we encounter day-to-day, or striking out on a family walk with a paper map and a compass, instead of relying on GPS on phones.

Our brains can also store huge quantities of information if we train them. Instead of always using your device to search for or store the information you need, try this simple memory technique. The ancient Greeks used it to learn new speeches, and it can be applied to any situation where you need to memorize large amounts of information, such as remembering a to-do list or learning a presentation you're giving at work. It can also serve as a highly effective revision technique for any younger members of the family who are taking exams.

1. Think of a journey you do frequently that has several familiar locations along the way.

2. List the things you want to remember and think of a relevant image for each item on your list that will remind you of that item.

3. Mentally walk along the journey and "leave" each image at the familiar points on your route. Think of a way to connect each image with its location.

4. To recall all the items, visualize walking along your familiar route, "seeing" the images along the way.

3

FANTASY SENTENCES

We use online search engines, thesauruses, and dictionaries if we're ever stuck for words. And there's evidence that our use of language is suffering: emojis, text-speak, and communicating solely with images are replacing carefully crafted sentences. But spoken communication is still essential to us in our daily lives. Without a strong grasp of language and vocabulary we lose our ability to communicate well in interviews, at work and school, and when we're socializing. We need to combat the laziness that can set in when we don't have to find the right words to express ourselves, and boost our ability to be creative with language.

Try playing this game to help you reach into the recesses of your vocabulary and strengthen your verbal abilities. David Bowie used this technique to help inspire his song writing and to generate some of his unusual and eclectic word combinations.

1. Cut up individual words from the widest variety of magazines and newspapers you can find. Even consider cutting up old books that you might be

throwing out. Look for the widest variety of topics, styles, and writing techniques in your material.

2. Add to this pile of cut-up words some handwritten words, also on individual pieces of paper. These could include words you particularly like, or maybe an unusual word you learned only recently.

3. Put all the words into a basket or box. Make sure the individual pieces of paper are all folded carefully so that you can't glimpse the words from the outside.

4. Take it in turns to hand round the box and pull out three pieces of paper. Give everyone a set period of time, say two minutes, to form a coherent sentence using the three words that they have unfolded and extra words to make the sentence make sense. Say your sentences out loud to everyone in the group.

5. Award prizes for the sentences that are the most accomplished, interesting, or just plain hilarious.

"We need to . . .
boost our ability
to be creative
with language."

4

TAKE A BREAK

There's no escaping the fact that family life, fun though it is, can be very noisy. Living so close to other people, all at different stages in their lives and with different interests, means that peace and quiet can sometimes be very hard to find.

The presence of so many digital devices at home doesn't help our family noise levels. With so many notifications across hundreds of apps on all the devices we own, the constant demands on our attention and focus can be draining.

Press pause on the constant sensory stimulation by escaping to a dark, quiet room for 10 minutes of peace and calm. Choose a time when everyone is out of the house, or warn them in advance that they'll need to steer clear of the room you're in and keep noise just outside it to a minimum.

Practice sitting alone in the quiet and dark for a few minutes each day.

Don't try and meditate—just be alone with your thoughts.

Savor and enjoy the experience of silence.

Unplug your brain from all the constant stimulation around you and let it rest and recharge.

CHAPTER

7

LIFE
OFFSCREEN

Time away from the non-stop demands of our digital lives restores and refreshes us. Improvements in sleep, happiness, and stress levels are things we can each expect with longer periods of time offscreen. At home, switching off can be the perfect opportunity to rediscover activities that the whole family can enjoy, so we can really appreciate our time together. But it's been so long since any of us relied on anything *other* than screens to entertain us that the prospect of going screen-free for longer than an hour or so may seem rather daunting initially. What on earth will we do with all that time?

Some members of the family may need some convincing that "analogue" activities can have the entertainment power of an absorbing few hours spent on a screen. Others will view the idea of screen-free entertainment as hopelessly outdated. But through a bit of trial and error and the willingness to step out of your collective comfort zones, I can guarantee that you will find some new family activities (or rediscover old ones) that even the most cynical at home can enjoy.

Make it a family project to get everyone brainstorming screen-free activities to try together. These could include something one of you has always wanted to do, or something that one of you loves and would like to get the rest of you involved with. It might be a trip to a particular place, or it could be a skill you want to learn or an obscure sport to try. Let everyone take a hand in planning some screen-free activities, and discover how these can be just as entertaining as technology—and much more rewarding. In this section there are some ideas that you can try out, or that may inspire you to think of others.

DO YOU HAVE

A FULL "OFFSCREEN"

LIFE AT HOME?

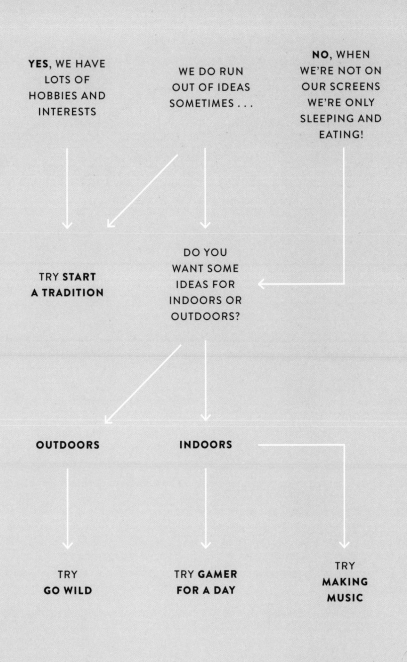

YES, WE HAVE
LOTS OF
HOBBIES AND
INTERESTS

WE DO RUN
OUT OF IDEAS
SOMETIMES . . .

NO, WHEN
WE'RE NOT ON
OUR SCREENS
WE'RE ONLY
SLEEPING AND
EATING!

TRY **START
A TRADITION**

DO YOU
WANT SOME
IDEAS FOR
INDOORS OR
OUTDOORS?

OUTDOORS

INDOORS

TRY
GO WILD

TRY **GAMER
FOR A DAY**

TRY
**MAKING
MUSIC**

1

MAKING MUSIC

The digital world appears to have largely stopped the family battles that used to happen over the volume of music playing in bedrooms. Our homes are often eerily quiet, each person with their headphones plugged in, lost in their own world, and listening to their choice of music without disturbing anyone else.

But music, and conversations about music, can bring generations together. In family homes when someone younger discovers a "new" song and it's pointed out that it's a cover version, or when an old band comes back into fashion and those older can reminisce about seeing them live—these are fun conversations to have.

To experience how a shared love of music can bond you all together, try sharing your music with each other instead of listening through headphones. Use the following ideas to help you plan a week of family musical experiences.

DINNER DJ

Take it in turns to provide the soundtrack for the family evening meal. Get everyone to put together a playlist and introduce the rest of the family to artists and tracks that they're enjoying. Some nights may be more successful than others, but remember—*everyone* gets a go.

MOBILE MUSIC

During all family car journeys for one week, ban individual headphones and music players, and take it in turns to choose the radio station you play each day, or split station choices up throughout a particular car trip.

CONCERT GOING

Find a live band playing nearby and organize a family outing to go and see them. It doesn't have to be a famous artist or an expensive venue—a small act playing locally can be just as fun.

"Take it in turns to provide the soundtrack for the family evening meal."

2

GAMER FOR A DAY

Computer and smartphone games offer us an escape from the stresses of our everyday lives, and combined with the dopamine rewards that they are designed to give us, it's not surprising why they can be so addictive. But many screen games are solitary challenges or involve playing against, and with, total strangers. Offscreen games give us an alternative. They provide us with absorbing imaginary worlds without the negative effects of too much screen time, as well as the opportunity to create memories as a family.

Find some offscreen board games that inspire and entertain everyone. There's a tendency in families to play games only during a holiday or on a special occasion, but for this challenge have a family gaming session midweek, or for no particular reason.

Take it in turns to choose the game.

Set a time limit for playing.

Agree that everyone tries everyone else's choice at least once, with no complaints.

Appoint someone to check the rules and explain how to play.

Get stuck in!

There are now many different styles of board games and imaginative themes to choose from, and something to suit any interest. Once you have found two or three games that you agree you all enjoy playing, make a family leader board that will be the alternative to the "highest scorer" league tables of online games, and keep it in the kitchen or a family space. The added element of competition will keep everyone coming back, helping to reduce the amount of time you each spend individually on your screens.

"Find some offscreen
board games that inspire
and entertain everyone."

3

START A TRADITION

Each family has traditions that only *they* do when they're all together, and that other families may not quite "get." As part of your time away from screens, get creative and make some new family traditions. Regular activities that you all look forward to and make time for will make screen-free time that much more appealing and successful. Here are some suggestions to get you thinking.

FRIDAY FEAST

Make it a Friday-night tradition that you take it in turns to get a takeaway and bring it back for everyone at home. Eat straight from the boxes to make the lack of washing-up part of the appeal.

SUMMER SCRAPBOOKS

Encourage children to make a scrapbook during the school vacation or when you're abroad on a family holiday. It doesn't have to be complicated—a cheap blank book will be suitable, and it can be filled with postcards, tickets, and drawings.

FAMILY SPORTS DAY

Once a year make it a family tradition to play competitive sports, such as baseball or five-a-side soccer. If your family is big enough you may not need to involve anyone else, but if not, how about inviting family friends to take part in your tournament? Each family could take turns hosting so you have "home" and "away" fixtures in your sporting calendar.

"GAVE IT A TRY" MEDAL

No matter how old we are, sometimes it's hard to challenge ourselves to try new things. To reward the effort made when someone tries a new food, a new activity (such as speaking in public), or anything else previously shied away from, create a family "gave it a try" medal. It's easy to find stores where you can customize the medal and ribbon with your family name.

4

GO WILD

Images of adventure and exploration are among the most popular types of pictures searched for on social media. We all love to see people, often complete strangers, challenging themselves in unfamiliar situations. From the comfort of our armchairs we can scroll through astonishing outdoor feats in beautiful locations and wonder wistfully what life would be like if we were out exploring the wild.

In fact, adventures can be accessible right outside your own front door—you don't need to travel thousands of miles to find them. Instead of pouring over other people's adventures on-screen, strike out on a family adventure of your own. Go camping and sleep outdoors under canvas for just one night, even if it's just in your back garden.

Split up the responsibility for planning and carrying out your adventure into distinct tasks and dole these out among you so that you're working together as a team.

Find a suitable location to walk or drive to and camp at.

**Pack (or maybe buy) the tent for you all
to sleep in.**

**Plan the meal and bring the supplies and
cooking equipment.**

Take charge of building the campfire.

Organize the evening entertainment.

Don't be too ambitious the first time you attempt a night
camping out. You might want to stay somewhere quite near
to home so you can dash back if you discover you've forgotten
something really quite essential (like an extra layer of clothes).
Try to keep an eye on the weather forecast leading up to your
campout, to ensure it's not too challenging for your first time.

When you've arrived at your destination, set up the tent, and
cooked and eaten the meal, sit around the campfire and enjoy
whatever entertainment your camp compère has planned—
roasting marshmallows might go down well, or a ghost story
telling competition.

Or just sit around the fire watching the flames flicker,
reconnecting with the people you love and who always have
your back, the group of people with whom you always feel at
home wherever you are—your family.

"Sit around the campfire and enjoy."